CHILDREN IN CRISIS

Living on the
Street

Hamilton's Story

Colin Hynson

WORLD ALMANAC® LIBRARY

Please visit our web site at: www.worldalmanaclibrary.com
For a free color catalog describing World Almanac® Library's list of high-quality books and multimedia programs, call 1-800-848-2928 (USA) or 1-800-387-3178 (Canada). World Almanac® Library's fax: (414) 332-3567.

Library of Congress Cataloging-in-Publication Data

Hynson, Colin.
   Living on the street: Hamilton's story / by Colin Hynson.
     p. cm. — (Children in crisis)
   Includes bibliographical references and index.
   ISBN 0-8368-5961-8 (lib. bdg.)
   1. Street children—Brazil—Juvenile literature. 2. Street children—Brazil—Biography—Juvenile literature. 3. Rodrigues, Hamilton Correia—Juvenile literature. 4. Poor children—Brazil—Social conditions—Juvenile literature. I. Title. II. Children in crisis (Milwaukee, Wis.)
   HV887.B8H96   2005
   362.7'086'9420981—dc22   2005047521

This North American edition first published in 2006 by
World Almanac® Library
A Member of the WRC Media Family of Companies
330 West Olive Street, Suite 100
Milwaukee, WI 53212 USA

World Almanac® Library managing editor: Valerie J. Weber
World Almanac® Library art direction: Tammy West
World Almanac® Library cover design and layout: Dave Kowalski
World Almanac® Library production: Jessica Morris

Photo credits: (t=top; b=bottom): Corbis 17t, 17b, 27b, 29b, 31b, 35b; Nivaldo Ferreira da Silva 25t, 37t; Exile Images 9t, 27t, 45b; Impact Photos 25b, 33b; Julia McNaught 1, 3, 8, 10, 12, 13t, 14, 16, 18, 19t, 20, 22, 24, 26, 28, 30, 31t, 32, 34, 36, 38; Magnum Photos 39t; Still Pictures 11b, 21t, 23b, 29t, 33t, 35t, 39b, 40; Hamilton Correia Rodrigues 3; World Image Library 4, 5b, 6, 7, 9b, 11t, 13b, 15t, 15b, 19b, 21b, 23t, 37b, 41t, 41b, 42, 43, 44, 45t.

Printed in the United States of America

1 2 3 4 5 6 7 8 9 09 08 07 06 05

The Interviewers

Julia McNaught from Estrela and Nivaldo Ferreira da Silva from Cultura em Movimento (Culture in Movement)—both based in Salvador, Brazil—conducted the interview with Hamilton, the subject of this book. Estrela is a British charity that works alongside and supports Brazilian youths and disadvantaged groups. Cultura em Movimento is a prominent reggae and cultural organization that stages many events in the Rocinha area of Salvador.

Elanor Jackson of ChildHope UK coordinated the interview. ChildHope has started many projects that strive to prevent poverty, conflict, and disease, hoping to improve life for young people.

Julia says: *"Doing the groundwork for this book has revived many happy memories. It has also revived my conviction about the importance of ensuring that there are opportunities for young people who are so full of creativity, sensitivity, hope, and a sense of freedom. Our world today needs people like them."*

Elanor says: *"Reading Hamilton's story a few years after ChildHope first knew him as a boy provides a sense of hope for other street children. For in spite of all the hardships he has suffered, Hamilton displays such resilience, generosity, and creativity—qualities that many more fortunate young people in the world lack."*

Julia McNaught and Nivaldo Ferreira da Silva (known artistically as Aluminio) conducted the interview with Hamilton.

CONTENTS

Introduction

Throughout the world, large numbers of children live on the streets. Many of them do not have a family's love and support in a safe home. Many street children must work in dangerous jobs, beg, or steal to survive. They often face attacks from other children and adults; some are even murdered. Every day, these children confront danger and disease; some of them will lose their fight for survival.

Children who live on the streets face many threats. Friends often stick together, choosing safety in numbers.

WHO ARE THE STREET CHILDREN?

It is impossible to know for certain exactly how many street children there are in Brazil at any one time. Millions of Brazilian children loosely called *street children* have quite different individual circumstances, placing them in several different categories. For example, *home-based children* is a term often used to define children who spend a significant proportion of their time on the streets but who still have family homes that they can go to for support and as a place to get

meals and sleep. These children spend their days—or nights—working on the streets to help support themselves and their families.

Homeless children live and work on the streets generally because they have run away from their homes and do not feel they can return. They might have left their families to escape poverty or because a family member was hurting them.

Another group live and work on the streets because, for whatever reason, the ties between the children and their parents have been cut. These children can often be found in war-torn countries or where poverty is so great that parents find it impossible to care for their children.

WHY TAKE TO THE STREETS?

Children are on the streets for all sorts of reasons. The main reason is simply that they come from a very poor background. They need to work to buy food and other essentials for themselves and their families. Other children are escaping from homes that are overcrowded. They may also be running away from domestic conflicts such as fights between parents or because their parents or other family members have forced them to leave. In times of war or civil conflicts, some children are separated from their parents or become orphans and have no extended family or anyone else to turn to.

Countries with the Highest Number of Street Children Worldwide

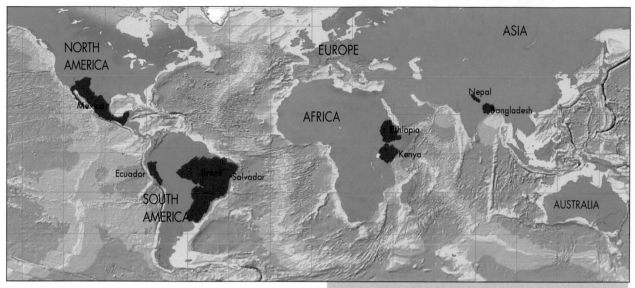

LIVING AND WORKING ON THE STREETS

Children on the streets can do many different kinds of jobs. The more straightforward—though poorly paid—jobs include washing cars, shining shoes, and running errands for store owners and others. Some of the jobs street children perform can be dangerous, including prostitution and carrying drugs.

Sleeping on the streets is a harsh reality for millions of children worldwide.

How Many Children Live on the Streets?

The precise number of children living on the streets is difficult to know. Some young-sters try to stay out of sight, undetected by police and social service agencies. Some live on the streets for a short time and then return home. Official estimates of the number of children worldwide who live on the streets either full- or part-time range from 100 million to 150 million. Latin America alone may have 40 million children living on its streets. The figures below are estimates.

Brazil	**7–8 million**
Bangladesh	**440,000**
Kenya	**250,000**
Ethiopia	**150,000**
Mexico	**114,000**
Nepal	**30,000**
Ecuador	**10,000**

Brazil is one of the most culturally diverse countries in the world. Brazilians descend from immigrants from a wide variety of countries, including Portugal and nations in Africa.

THE PEOPLE OF BRAZIL

The original Brazilians were Native American. Today, however, the majority of Brazilians are of Portuguese origin or are descended from African slaves. One-third of all Brazilians are mulattoes, meaning of mixed race, usually a blend of African and European. There are also a large number of Germans, Poles, Japanese, Italians, and Germans. More recently, people from Korea and the Middle East have moved to Brazil.

THE GROWTH OF BRAZIL'S CITIES

Brazil is rapidly becoming an urban society, as more people are born in the cities or move in from the countryside. People from the countryside come to the cities to escape poverty, attracted by the promise of a well-paid job and a better life. They bring their

BRAZIL: A BRIEF HISTORY

For centuries, Portugal controlled Brazil as its colony. In 1822, Brazil became independent. For many years, people in Brazil did not have many rights, and free speech was not allowed. Through most of the late twentieth century, a military dictatorship ruled Brazil. Then, in 1985, a civilian became president, sparking the beginning of democracy in Brazil. Human rights were gradually introduced. In 2002, Luiz Inácio Lula da Silva (known as Lula), the leader of the Workers' Party, was elected president.

Brazil is a land of great contrasts. It is the fifth largest country in the world and has the tenth largest economy, but the gap between rich and poor is one of the biggest in the world. The wealthiest 1 percent of Brazil's population controls nearly 50 percent of the country's wealth. The poorest 50 percent receives less than 10 percent of the country's income.

BRAZIL: FACTS AND FIGURES

Population:	**184 million**
Capital City:	**Brasília**
Geography:	**Largest country in South America. Mostly forests and lowlands with some plains and mountains**
Climate:	**Mostly tropical but cooler in the south**
Religions:	**About 80 percent of Brazilians are Roman Catholic, making the country the largest Roman Catholic nation in the world. The rest mostly belong to other Christian groups and African religions.**
Literacy:	**One-third of all Brazilians cannot read or write.**

Luxurious apartment buildings for the wealthy line ocean beaches.

large families, further increasing the cities' populations. Today, about 80 percent of all Brazilians live in urban areas. The United Nations estimates that by 2015, this will increase to nearly 90 percent. The sheer volume of new people severely strains the cities' ability to provide housing, jobs, and transportation. Many migrants remain poor, and their children find themselves on the streets.

THE STREET CHILDREN OF BRAZIL

In a country with so much poverty, it is not surprising that there are so many children living and working on the city streets. Many of the wealthier people living in the cities, however, do not feel sorry for these children. Instead, they see them as a nuisance and a threat to their way of life.

Many companies employ security guards to keep these children away from the areas where they do business. Police officers are also often intolerant of street children. This police attitude has prompted the emergence of "death squads"—groups of police officers who kill children just for being on the streets.

RECENT HISTORY TIMELINE

1964 The military overthrows Jõao Goulart, the elected president of Brazil. General Humberto Branco becomes the new leader of Brazil.

1968 Workers and students stage large demonstrations and strikes against the military government. The Roman Catholic Church sides with the protesters. The military responds by suspending civil liberties. Opposition leaders leave the country.

1969–1974 Brazil enjoys an economic boom. The world's largest hydroelectric dam is built. At the same time, the government heavily censors all newspapers, magazines, and television and radio programs and tortures and imprisons political opponents.

1979 Political activists, intellectuals, and people from the labor unions form the Workers' Party to oppose the military government.

1985 Democracy is restored to Brazil.

1989 Fernando Collor de Mello wins the first free and fair presidential election.

1992 President Collor is charged with corruption.

1993 Fernando Henrique Cardoso is elected president. Police officers kill eight street children in the Candelaria massacre.

2002 Lula, the leader of the Workers' Party, wins the presidential election. He promises political and economic reforms.

2003 Land reform begins with land being given to 400,000 poor families.

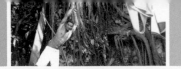

CHAPTER ONE: Meet Hamilton

Almost one-fourth of Brazil's population lives under the poverty line, earning less than eighty dollars per month. Desperation for money and food often drives the children of poor families onto the streets to beg or find some kind of employment. For young people, the streets can be a way of escaping the hardships of their home lives. Hamilton Rodrigues is a young person who has spent a great proportion of his life so far on the streets.

HAMILTON SAYS:

"My name is Hamilton Correia Rodrigues, and I am eighteen years old. I was born in Pelourinho in Salvador, Bahia, Brazil. I am nothing—since I began life, right up until today. But I am a person, a human being. I'm cool, humble, fun, and cheerful—that is what I am. I'm tall with black hair, now with designer details.

Other people see me as someone who does nothing in life. Adventuring into the day, selling something or other.

I can speak Portuguese and a little bit of Spanish, Italian, and English. I like studying, reading, and capoeira. My friends and I sometimes go to the beach for fun."

ALUMINIO SAYS:

"Hamilton is someone who had a very low life expectancy, but he's a survivor of the streets. He's back at home now, still working the streets, selling souvenirs and having a good time.

I don't see him as a bad kid—rebellious, but not offensive. His fight for survival corresponds to the way he has been brought up."

Hamilton is a thoughtful, intelligent young man with a lot of passion and enthusiasm for life.

DONA AURENITA (HAMILTON'S MOTHER) SAYS:

"Hamilton's my son. He used to run away from home, even in his underpants sometimes! He'd go after the vans with megaphones and loud music that would play those Carnival songs. Loads of kids would go after them. He gave me a lot of trouble; it was terribly hard to try and get him to come back. Sometimes I'd go after him with clothes—a T-shirt and shorts. When he started going on the streets, I'd go to the Youth Justice [courts that deal with young offenders], and once they told me he was in the juvenile lockup [detention]. I had many sleepless nights staying up and going after him."

HOME ON THE STREETS

It is estimated that about 20 million children spend a high proportion of their time on Brazil's city streets. This figure includes a high number of children who are on the streets during the day and return to their families at night. These children are usually working to bring some extra money to their poor parents. Besides these children who have a home, there is also an estimated 7 to 8 million children for whom the streets are their home—both day and night.

For many children on the streets, the streets are their playground. Few organized recreational activities are available.

Most children on the streets feel they have nobody to turn to for help or support.

THE DAILY STRUGGLE

Street children face a daily struggle for survival. Not only do they have to find money for food and other necessities for survival, but they also face many dangers on the streets.

While a large number of children succumb to the many traumas, threats, and diseases that threaten them, others survive and even carry on to create a better life for themselves. Living and/or working on the streets often instills an amazing resilience in these young people; many survive because of their strong character and determination to stay alive at all costs.

Living on the Street

HAMILTON SAYS:

"I can read and write a bit—enough to survive. I used to go to school, the Mestre Pastinha School, for about four years. I liked the kids, the teachers, the snacks, and playing around in the classroom. I also liked drawing. I didn't like tests though. I played truant loads—missed school to go and hang out and smoke on the streets. My favorite subjects were art and drawing. I'm actually thinking of going back to study more soon.

There was one really pretty teacher when I was at school. I saw her not so long ago, and she remembered me. My favorite book is by Jorge Amado. It's called Gabriela, Clove and Cinnamon. Amado writes all about Bahia, our history and culture.

My best friends are my mum, my dad, and my sister. I have a pretty good relationship with my family. My sister Bete and I are closest. We live together, we help each other. We fight, but we're close. My oldest sister Naná lives in another neighborhood with her husband and two children. We get on OK, but we're more distant. On the streets, my best friends were Jau (Jailton), Juquinha (Ricardo), and Itamar."

Hamilton at age twelve (*back*) poses with his friends, Isaias, Gabriela, and Moabe, from Project Ibveji. The friends were performing at a street-theater cultural event organized by Project Altivaçao.

EDUCATION IN BRAZIL

Education in Brazil is undergoing a crisis. According to Brazilian law, children between the ages of seven and fourteen must go to school. In practice, however, the law is impossible to enforce. The children of poor families are much less likely to finish their education than children of wealthy families.

For children living on the streets, going to school is even more difficult because they need to work during the day. In addition, no adults are on the streets to ensure they attend or have the right clothes and school supplies.

Currently, 4 million children in Brazil do not go to school. Only 40 percent of children who begin their primary education actually complete it. A vast difference also exists in the standards of teaching and facilities between private schools in wealthier districts and state schools in poverty-stricken areas.

The luxury of school lessons with an abundance of resources shown here is a far cry from the overcrowded classes with few books and school supplies available to children in slums.

Tourism is a major source of industry in Brazil's cities. Many street children make a living selling to travelers.

THE TOURIST INDUSTRY

Brazil is becoming more and more popular as a tourist destination. Many tourists come to Brazil to relax on the beaches or watch the carnivals. Ecotourists interested in nature often visit the Amazon jungle or the spectacular Iguacu Falls.

The number of people who come to Brazil for their vacation has risen from just over 1 million in 1990 to about 4 million in 2000. Nearly half of these visitors come from other South American countries, particularly neighboring Argentina. Tourism provides more than 6 million jobs, so it is a very important part of Brazil's economy. Many street children rely on a regular influx of tourists to provide them with business.

Living on the Street

"My family are Afro-Brazilian. I am passionate about many aspects of my culture, such as capoeira, samba, drumming, and percussion—all things that have a connection to Africa. Bahia is the second Africa. We have the largest black population outside Africa.

I know a bit about the history of our people. I know we're the descendants of slaves. My mother is from Jacobina, inland Bahia. I have always lived in Bahia; today I live in the Rocinha, one of Pelourinho's surviving ghettos.

The festivals we celebrate include Carnival, Saint John's Festival, New Year, and Christmas. At Carnival, there is lots of adrenalin! Lots of women, poppers, and music. I like going after the big trio elétricos (giant sound systems and bands on moving wagons) and having a good time.

I like to do all sorts of things with my friends. We used to play about on the streets or we'd go to the beach. The biggest adventure we ever had was when the police came after us and caught us; they'd seen us rob an old woman. They got hold of me and Jau by our shirts and were taking us off. I managed to wriggle my way out of my shirt, and the policeman ended up with my shirt in his hands! It was in Graça. When he realized, he let go of Jau, and he got away as well!

I knew a lot of lads who were involved in burglaries and wanted us to get involved, too. I would just get up and go away when they started talking about it.

I believe in God, God in the heart, and I pray every night. I don't go to church regularly anymore. I used to go to the Baptist Church with my mother when I was little. However, it's no longer there.

For me, Jesus is the salvation, of all problems. God is salvation. I believe that when a person dies, they see the book of their life. They then have to pay for what they did in their life on Earth—the good and the bad. Each person will then get what they deserve.

I am a person who likes to look for the good side in everything. I try and do good things, and I try to be peaceful and calm as much as possible.

I often imagine what it would be like to have a house of my own. The house of my life. In my own home, I would be able to live with my wife and raise my child like anybody, a worker. And my

Despite all the hardships he has endured, Hamilton remains passionate about his family and his culture.

12

Hamilton, age twelve (third from left), and other members of Ibveji's theater group prepare to join a march against racial violence and death squads.

mother would live there too, if she's alive, God willing. Living with my mum makes me happy. Funny people also make me happy. People who are natural jokers or clowns; they really make me laugh. I like their attitude.

The happiest day of my life was when I was in Morro de São Paulo [a tropical island beach resort] with four Spaniards, a caipirinha cocktail in my hand, and fifteen hundred reals [equal to six hundred U.S. dollars] in my pocket!

I adore music . . . 'streetkids selling ice lollies, streetkids cleaning windscreens' [lyrics from a carnival song]. I was part of Buscapé [a children's carnival group]. I used to play with Mestre Prego and the Banda Meninos do Pelô—samba percussion; I would play the big drums."

FACTS: FESTIVALS AND CARNIVAL

Brazilians celebrate a wide variety of religious and nonreligious festivals every year. Thousands flock to the streets to witness and join in with music, dancing, costumes, and public religious ceremonies.

• Every June in Brazil, Roman Catholics remember Saints Anthony, Peter, and John with huge outdoor firework parties known as *festas juninas.*

• Many festivals are celebrated by those who follow the African faith known as Candomblé. These highly ritualized events involve animal sacrifices, ceremonial clothing, dances, and songs.

• In Salvador, the Lavagem do Bonfim festival has been celebrated every January since 1754. During this festival, a group of women dress completely in white and carry long, white vases on their heads filled with perfumed water and white flowers.

• The most famous nonreligious carnival in Brazil during February and March is Carnival. People come from all over to enjoy the spectacle. The biggest parties take place in Salvador and Rio de Janeiro. The costumes, parades, music, and partying all contribute to making Brazil the Carnival capital of the world.

During Carnival, groups of dancers and singers perform on the streets in routines they have practiced for months.

Living on the Street

"Loads of people lived on the streets like I did. I have four friends who lived on the streets with me, but there are many more. The good things about living on the streets were the friends and freedom. I liked playing about and being cheeky [sassy] with the others. Most of all, the excitement is what appeals. The cold and the rain is probably the hardest thing.

We never really lived in one place on the street, but rather we moved around a bit. I hung about in Campo Grande, Canela, Graça, Barra, and Piedade—all central and wealthier districts of Salvador because otherwise my mother would catch me. I hung around with my friends Jau, Juquinha, and Itamar. We used to sleep on top of bus shelters, behind kiosks, on the beach, or in the park. It would depend which neighborhood we were in. We used to eat leftovers—of hamburgers, chips [french fries], juice, pop. We used to go down to Lapa central bus station and get hot dogs. We'd beg them from people or ask for a bite, and if they didn't give us them, we'd just snatch them and run!

I feel angry when I speak and the person ignores me and doesn't pay any attention. There was no shortage of that when I was a kid. I hate people talking badly about one another. When I am sad or angry, I talk to my sister Bete. I am generally a calm and happy person.

I like playing capoeira and swimming in the sea. And playing a bit of football [soccer] sometimes, but I'm best at capoeira."

For fun, Hamilton likes capoeira, a kind of martial art that requires grace, agility, and concentration.

RECREATION IN BRAZIL

The people of Brazil are passionate about sports, and they are particularly enthusiastic about soccer. Street children often play soccer in the favelas, in public squares, and on the beaches of Rio de Janeiro. Pelé, Brazil's greatest soccer hero, is regarded internationally as the greatest soccer player of all time, inspiring many young Brazilians to follow in his footsteps. People also play volleyball, the second favorite sport of Brazil, on beaches. Other popular sports include tennis, basketball, and surfing.

Each city has its own public holidays, which are usually an excuse for everybody in the city, young and old, to mingle and enjoy themselves. Brazilians really know how to throw a party!

It is often said that in Brazil, volleyball is the most popular sport. Soccer, they say, doesn't count as sport because it is considered a religion!

The unique sport known as capoeira is one of the most popular pastimes among young Brazilians.

WHAT IS CAPOEIRA?

Capoeira is a type of martial art created by African slaves in Brazil about four hundred years ago. Much more than a martial art, capoeira is a powerful, graceful performance somewhere between a choreographed acrobatic dance and a noncontact fight between two players. Music also plays an integral part in the game of capoeira.

Capoeira was originally designed as a symbolic representation of slaves rising up against their oppressors. People who play capoeira must be very fit and strong while also having all the grace of a dancer.

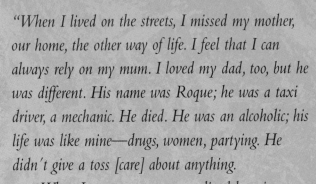

"When I lived on the streets, I missed my mother, our home, the other way of life. I feel that I can always rely on my mum. I loved my dad, too, but he was different. His name was Roque; he was a taxi driver, a mechanic. He died. He was an alcoholic; his life was like mine—drugs, women, partying. He didn't give a toss [care] about anything.

When I was very young, we lived here in Pelourinho, in Maciel, until the government moved us out. Our house looked out onto what is now Pedro Arcanjo Square. They have big music and dance shows for tourists there now.

I remember a whole load of police came round to give notice. Going from house to house, aggressively, saying that on such and such a day, we would get our money. They were taking people's names down on paper and telling us the date we had to be out.

That was the first round of evicting the people of Pelourinho for tourist developments. When we were evicted, we moved down to Gravatá (a nearby neighborhood). When the compensation money came through, my dad took it and left. He left us with nothing. I was about six years old then."

ALUMINIO SAYS:

"At the end of the 1980s, the [government] authorities appeared with this story about housing restoration. It began at the bottom of Taboão, the lower area of Pelourinho. It soon became apparent that they were giving residents one thousand reals, or

This is one of the big, old ruined houses in Pelourinho. This district was the location of slave auctions before the early nineteenth century, when slavery was still legal in Brazil.

even only eight hundred, and taking their houses away from them, saying they would reform [restore] them and once they were reformed, they would give them back to residents.

About 1 percent of people were given other houses on the periphery of the city. Another 1 percent bought themselves a piece of land. The rest of them, the majority, ended up under bridges and viaducts, on the city streets, in cardboard boxes. Most people didn't know what to do. Hamilton's family was moved out in this first round of evictions for restoration."

More than two hundred different ethnic groups co-exist in Brazil, resulting in a rich cultural heritage.

PEOPLE AND CULTURE

Brazil is a country that is proud of its multiethnic nature. This cultural diversity is visible in its variety of art styles, music, dance, crafts, kinds of food, and other traditions.

Brazilian cuisine is heavily influenced by its varied cultural mix. The country's national dish consists of rice, black beans, and either meat or fish. This meal is called *feijoada*.

Many charcteristics also unite the diverse peoples of Brazil. For example, 170 of the country's 184 million people speak Portuguese, the national language. Many residents also follow the Catholic faith brought by the original Portuguese settlers.

BAHIA AND SALVADOR

The people of the state of Bahia revel in their rich cultural mix; a significant part of its population is of African descent. Salvador is Bahia's capital and the third largest city in Brazil.

The Pelourinho district in Salvador has the largest collection of baroque architecture in Latin America and is a United Nations Educational, Scientific and Cultural Organization World Heritage site. The colorful buildings and cobblestone streets perfectly complement the many other vibrant elements of this cultural mecca.

Colorful houses mingle with older colonial architecture in Salvador. The city was Brazil's colonial capital.

17

CHAPTER TWO: The Hardships of Home

Growing up in poverty can mean that home—whether in a house or on the streets—can be a troublesome environment for many children and adolescents. For children with unhappy home lives, the streets can seem like a way of running away from their problems and the chance to earn some money at first. Reality soon sets in, though, in the form of cold nights, endless hunger, and long hours of work for very little pay.

Hamilton left home because he saw the streets as a way to freedom, to escape reality.

HAMILTON SAYS:

"When I was a little kid, I used to go to a place called Criançarte (Kid Art) at the Terreiro de Jesus with a bunch of other kids. We'd do activities; that was before I went on to the streets.

It was after my father left and we had moved to Gravatá that I began to run away from home to the streets. I was about six. The Youth Justice would pick me up, and my mum would come after me. I'm from a low-class family. Mum was a good mother, but there was nothing she could do to stop me running away. I left home so I could hang out with street kids, smoke cigarettes and cannabis, and sniff glue.

After being on the streets for a period, some other kids told me that Criançarte had changed to the Ibveji Project in Rua Chile. So I went along there. At the project, we'd get

Belonging to groups like the Ibveji Project gives children like Hamilton (second from left) a sense of belonging when they have severed ties with their families.

paid five reals [two dollars] a week if we attended school, so I went back to school, to the Mestre Pastinha School.

I loved it at Project Ibveji; there I would eat, drink, and sleep. I was a street kid, I wasn't interested in anything else, just the basics. After a little while, I left everything again, and went back to the streets.

What I liked most there was theater— a play that we did about a street kid selling on the streets. The play was simple and practical; it caught my attention, I really liked it. I'd like to do more with the theater sometime. I liked the coconut workshop, too; we made coconut buttons, rings, hairclips, bags, bikinis."

FACTS: POVERTY IN BRAZIL

Brazil has one of the highest rates of poverty in the world, including an alarmingly high rate of child poverty. The statistics speak for themselves:

• In 2004, it was estimated that 44 million Brazilians were living below the international poverty line.

• The minimum wage in Brazil is one U.S. dollar a day. Fifty-eight million Brazilians survive on this. Many others survive on less.

• The poorest 10 percent of Brazil's population owns only 0.7 percent of Brazil's wealth. The richest 10 percent control 48 percent.

• One in three of the people of Rio de Janeiro live in slums called favelas. The largest favela is home to more than 150,000 people. It lies in the heart of the wealthy neighborhood of Gávea.

• Three children under the age of five die in Brazil every five minutes. More than 100,000 children die before their first birthday.

Millions of Brazilians live in crowded, slumlike conditions in the poorer parts of the country.

Living on the Street

"Later, I lived at Project Ibveji for a while. After that, I started to go home. The people at Project Ibveji helped me a lot. If it hadn't been for Ibveji, I wouldn't be the person I am now. They offered me a way to get away from the streets.

When I left Ibveji, I was about thirteen or fourteen. I was back at home by then. That was when I broadened my horizons a bit. I liked to dress well then. I would go to school dressed in really smart casual gear, shoes, the lot. Ibveji had set me up with it. I really used to go to school then.

A bit later, I went back to the house my mother had rented in Gravatá. However, when I got there, I found she wasn't living there anymore. My God, I got a fright! Eventually I found out that she'd moved up the road to another place. I found her, and she took me in there. Unfortunately, my mother hadn't been able to manage to keep paying rent, and we didn't have any food, so she had to leave that place, and then we were all on the streets for several days.

Next, my mother went and made a one-room shack inside the shell of a big, old, ruined house. Only the front façade of the house was standing, which is common in the historical center. I was living on the streets at the time; I didn't live with her there.

Then I decided to go back to Ibveji, and I began to study again. That was when I got to know the gang—Juquinha, Jau, and Itamar. We would sell chocolates and sweets [candies] in the streets and on the buses. I used to go to their houses, too, in their neighborhoods and sleep there sometimes. Itamar lived in Barros Reis, and Jau lived in Sete de Abril."

Despite his years on the streets when his mother didn't know where he was some of the time, Hamilton and his mother are very close today.

DRIVEN OUT OF HOME

In poorer parts of Brazil, the average number of people living in each household is eight. Children from these large families work on the streets to make money to take home.

There are many reasons why children make the streets their home. Sometimes, parents simply cannot cope with the number of people they must feed and send their children away. Some children do not get the attention or love they need, so they leave to look for something better. Conflict between children and parents can lead to young people running away. Some children are also victims of domestic violence and/or sexual abuse. Poverty also creates other tensions that lead to children leaving home.

Large families living in poverty sometimes willingly send their children out to work in a desperate attempt to increase the family income.

DISEASE AND ILLNESS

More than 70 percent of Brazil's poor have no access to clean running water, refrigeration,

Brazilians who live on the streets and in sprawling slums are often forced to drink dirty water that spreads many preventable diseases.

or sewage disposal. This is a big problem in the slums, creating the right environment for diseases to spread. Most diseases common in poverty-stricken areas, such as malaria, can easily be prevented with improvements such as clean, running water and adequate sewers.

It is estimated that more than 40 million people in Brazil do not eat well. The poor, particularly street children, do not have a way to cook their own food, and they cannot always afford to buy their meals. Because of inadequate food and poor nutrition, the average height of a Brazilian woman is the same as that of a twelve-year-old girl in Europe or North America.

"A favela is a poor community of houses made of planks. There's more despair there, it's heavier. There's more robbery and thieving. Engomadeira— a favela I know—that's one life. Nobody can say much. Nobody can play loud music, disobey, bother neighbors. If you do, there are problems—dodgy [quesionable, tricky] people, craftiness. You either leave or die. If you're lucky, they'll let you leave running. The Rocinha is a ghetto, but it's different. It's very green and much calmer.

The wealthier suburbs are full of police and people in ties and suits. Chic buildings. The rich kids live there—people who have the money to do what they like."

JULIA SAYS:

"Family breakdown is a major factor that pushes children from poorer backgrounds toward the streets in Bahia, as we can see from Hamilton's story. The lack of paternal responsibility, and often new stepfathers on the scene, creates a difficult social and economic situation. These circumstances are not uncommon in other parts of the world, be it Britain or Brazil. It is time we looked closer at some of the similarities we have in our different cultures, to see where we are all going wrong, and how we can start putting an end to the unnecessary difficulties we create for children and young people—be it at home or around our cities."

Today, Hamilton has a good relationship with his sister Bete. This photo was taken in Rocinha, where they both live.

THE FAVELAS

Brazil is a country of extremes. While there is great wealth and beauty in the cities and countryside, there is also a great deal of poverty. The families of many of Brazil's street children live in parts of cities known as favelas. *Favela* refers to the shantytowns that have grown up around the edges of cities. They started to appear as families began to move from the countryside to find work in the cities. It was not until the 1990s that efforts began to improve the favelas with street lighting and garbage collection.

They still do not have the same services as other parts of the city, however. Many homes lack electricity for lighting, refrigeration, and telephones. Power shortages are frequent. Favela inhabitants often have little access to hospitals, police services, and public or private transportation.

Favela houses are built from cheap materials on steep slopes. They are often in danger of tumbling down.

DEATH ON THE STREETS

The number of children dying in Brazil is much higher than that in many other countries. Part of the reason for this is simply that children make up a huge percentage of the population in Brazil. Another reason for the high death toll is that poor children, especially street children, in Brazil are more likely to be undernourished and vulnerable to disease. Street children also run the risk of being killed either by other children or by adults.

Many of the adults in Brazil who might be expected to look after these children, such as police officers or security guards, are actually trying to clear them off the streets. They often use violence and even murder to clear away these children for the sake of the rest of the town.

More than one hundred Brazilians are shot and killed on the city streets every day, some of them children.

CHAPTER THREE: Multiple Threats

Children on the streets must constantly keep their wits about them because a huge number of dangers and people threaten their daily existence—from disease, murder, and violence to drugs, prostitution, and corrupt authorities. The younger these youths are, the greater the risk that they will be caught up in something dangerous to their health, well-being, and even their lives. Children and teenagers are easy prey for drug gangs looking for runners, while prostitution can seem like an easy way of making money at first.

HAMILTON SAYS:

"Going to sleep and waking up with the same things—it's a story that leaves me sad. Hunger is what makes me cry. When I've got no money for food and there's nothing at home. That's what really gets to me. We are day-by-day people, we're adventurers. I last cried at New Year. Giving thanks for another year of life and health, hoping for a new life. My most precious possession is my health.

The saddest day of my life occurred when the military police strike was on. Me and Jau were breaking into a shop, and he got shot in the stomach. I thought I was losing my friend. Thank God he didn't die though.

Hamilton is shown here with Marcos Paulo, a young boy not unlike a younger version of himself from his neighborhood.

Some children play in Rocinha, the district where Hamilton now lives with his mother.

It's worse for girls on the street than boys. There's more risk for girls of being raped or sexually abused. Everyone looks out for themselves on the streets. You're part of a group up until a certain point. When it comes to food—each one for himself! We sleep together. The police often wake us up.

When I lived on the streets, I would go to the toilet in the bushes, in old abandoned houses, behind cars, or in bars. We rarely had baths. We used to hang about really dirty! We only got clean when we went for a swim at the beach. I didn't wash much and we often wore the same clothes. I try to stay fit and healthy now. I don't know if I know anyone who is HIV positive or who has AIDS, that is, people don't know or don't say."

FACTS: PREGNANCY AND HIV

With little health care, people living in the slums and on the streets of Brazil are at high risk for the spread of disease, unwanted pregnancies, and threats to new mothers and their babies:

• It is estimated that about 2 million children between the ages of ten and fifteen are involved in prostitution.

• About 18 percent of all fifteen- to nineteen-year-old girls are pregnant or already mothers.

• Of all the new babies born in Brazil, about 1 percent are to mothers between the ages of ten and fourteen.

• For every one thousand births, about thirty babies will die soon after being born.

• About 21 percent of boys living on the street have had sex with another man or boy.

• Brazil has the highest number of people with HIV/AIDS in Latin America. More than one-half million people in Brazil have HIV.

Girls on the streets working as prostitutes are particularly at risk of unwanted pregnancies and contracting sexually transmitted diseases.

Living on the Street

"I've had a few girlfriends. I've got a tattoo on my arm—the name of an Israeli girlfriend.

Drugs are easy to get hold of in Salvador and yet quite expensive. There are lots of drug gangs on our streets; I think they are a real problem. I do know some people who work for them. I used to be really scared of them. I'd leave and go elsewhere whenever I saw them. They used to tell us they killed street kids.

I know people in the favela and in Pelourinho [the city's center] who have died working for drug gangs. People get killed by these gangs because they get drugs and then don't pay for them, and the guys get angry and kill them.

When I lived on the streets, I was always getting beaten up by heavy groups. I'd get beaten up all over. I used to beat other kids up, too. Sometimes for money that they owed me, or for taking the mickey out of [insulting] me.

I wasn't really part of a street gang when I lived on the streets. There was just a bunch of us that hung out together a lot. We'd try and stick together. Other kids on the street liked our group because we used to play jokes, have fun, and get up to mischief.

I used to try and avoid fights; I would just leave if I could. We used to each carry a bit of broken glass around to defend ourselves. And we were always pinching [stealing] small knives."

Hamilton grins in his bedraoom at home. He prefers staying there to trying to find a place on the streets, where drug gangs threaten people.

DRUG GANGS

Gangs that deal drugs will always try to protect their territory so other gangs cannot do business there. They control many favelas. Often the police will not attempt to enforce law and order in these areas so the drug gangs take on that role. In return, they expect loyalty from their members and young people to do any jobs they are asked to do. These jobs can range from keeping lookout to carrying messages to becoming armed gang members ready to defend their territory. Members of drug gangs kill two to three police officers every week.

Young people cannot be arrested in Brazil unless they are actually caught committing a crime. This law makes them ideal candidates for carrying drugs from one person to another. An armed gang member can earn about five hundred dollars a month—a lot more than many legal jobs.

This boy poses with the gun he received for being a member of a drug gang.

SELLING SEX

With limited options available to them for making money, street children often resort to selling sex for cash. It is usually girls who turn to prostitution; however, many boys become prostitutes as well. Some street children have resorted to having sex with police officers in return for protection or because the police officers force them.

According to one study, Brazil has the highest rate of child prostitution in Latin America and the second highest rate in the world. It is estimated that there are 500,000 children involved in prostitution in Brazil. It is impossible to know the precise figure, however, because many of these young people feel ashamed of what they are doing and do not want to talk about it.

This eight-year-old girl is one of many children who turn to prostitution as a means of earning money on the streets of Brazil.

"I think drugs are a big problem in Brazil. In fact, in my opinion, drugs are the worst problem of everything that is wrong in the community. It disorganizes everything, and that's what leads us into poverty.

I used to get harassed by the police a lot; they'd catch us sniffing glue and beat us up. Then they would take us to CAM (the youth detention center) or the Youth Justice. I once spent two months in CAM. The police caught me with cannabis. It was before I went to the Ibveji Project; I was about eleven or twelve at the time. I used to carry drugs for dealers from one place to another, and that was how I got caught—the drugs weren't mine.

I'm not so much afraid of the police as afraid of their cowardly ways—the way they pick up on people's weak points and play dirty. I try to avoid the police. I just keep cool and quiet. Street children get raped by the police quite frequently; it happens a lot with girls. It happens with boys, too, but less often. I know of people who have been killed by the police, too, here in Pelourinho.

There are the occasional good police officers who care about street kids. Out of every ten nasty ones, there's one nicer one—a brother."

Hamilton sometimes had to resort to petty crime when he lived on the streets. He saw it as a necessary part of his life there.

CAN THE POLICE BE TRUSTED?

In 1997, the Brazilian congress set up a special commission to look into the problem of groups of police officers acting outside the law by killing those that they saw as a threat, particularly street children. The commission found that these groups—known as "death squads"—were active in many of Brazil's cities, especially in the favelas. Street children are most vulnerable to death squads because they have nowhere to escape to and nobody to protect them. Anyone, however, can be a victim of these squads.

Although these police officers are acting illegally and have killed many innocent people, (including an estimated two to five children each day), they get a lot of public support.

Many believe that street children are a menace to society and need to be cleared off the streets. In fact, sometimes local business owners and politicians pay for the murders.

Many Brazilian police officers are known to be corrupt. Most treat street children badly, with little regard for their welfare.

A MATTER OF SECURITY

Lethal attacks from security guards are one of the main dangers facing street children. A number of store owners believe that street children steal from them or deter customers from entering stores. They pay for security guards not only to watch over the stores but also to drive away any street children who are near their buildings.

Wealthier Brazilians who live in communities behind security fences and gates also employ security guards. They patrol the streets and chase away children who do not live there. These security guards may also go into the favelas at night and attack sleeping children. Many people illegally possess guns, hoping to protect themselves from crime. About forty thousand Brazilians are shot to death yearly, one of the world's highest death rates from firearms.

This woman owns a handgun to protect her from people threatening her personal safety.

CHAPTER FOUR: Fight for Survival

Hamilton would be the first to admit that you need to be tough to survive in a world where drug gangs and aggressive police dominate. Becoming part of a gang can be one way for young people on the streets to feel more secure—ensuring there is always someone looking out for them. At first, drugs might seem to offer a distraction from the perpetual cold and hunger, but the ill effects are serious long-term health problems and addiction. Addiction can drive many desperate drug users to crime to support their habit.

HAMILTON SAYS:

"When I lived on the streets, my friends and I would share what we had with each other when any of us were hard up. Sometimes we would club together and put in one real each to buy a plate of food. Most of the time I would share with my friends, but not always

I have seen someone die before. We were at the Farol da Barra [lighthouse by the beach], having a smoke behind the rocks. Two guys were down on the beach shouting at each other. The first guy got this big rock and hurled it at the other guy's head. He went down there and then.

When street children do die, they'll be buried if they have families. I remember Laércio, a kid that used to hang out at Piedade Square. He was asleep. They killed him with a stone on his head. He was buried. His family went to his funeral.

Hamilton knows that life is cheap on the streets. He believes the best way to stay out of trouble is to walk away at the first sign of it.

Hamilton visits the home of Cultura em Movimento (Culture and Movement), an organization working at the heart of Rocinha's social and cultural movement.

I often dream about studying again. I would really like to be a mechanic; that was my father's profession. A normal job like that would really suit me, I think. Big businessmen inspire me.

If I was the president of Brazil, I would put an end to poverty. I would also put an end to hunger and get people off the streets. I'd also provide more medical assistance and more schooling."

FACTS: DRUGS IN BRAZIL

Street children can be easily drawn to drugs. Many act as drug smugglers or even take drugs themselves to help them cope with their difficult lives:

• In 1992, a survey of street children showed that 100 percent had tried drugs at one time.

• In 1991, a survey of street children in Sao Paolo revealed that 45 percent of them used drugs every day.

• Glue and marijuana are the most commonly used drugs among street children.

• Glue and similar substances are inhaled from plastic or glass bottles. These inhalants are highly addictive and very damaging to the brain.

• One of the substances that street children sniff is called *bim,* which is made from benzene. This drug can cause cancer, anemia, and harmful effects on the bone marrow and immune system when used for a long time.

• *Pasta de coca* is a paste that contains cocaine. Street children usually smoke it.

• Some drugs, like Rohypnol, are popular and legal. They can be bought in most drug stores.

Drug gangs control most of Rio de Janeiro's slums. Brazilian police patrol the Rocinha favela after a confrontation between rival drug gangs in 2004.

Living on the Street

"As for what I do to earn money, I sell craft necklaces to tourists. I got started selling necklaces when I first bought a dozen of them from the people who sell them in large quantities to vendors.

The necklaces were cheap to buy, and I could make up to fifty reals (twenty dollars) a day in the summer season. In the winter, it was really hard to make even five reals (two dollars), sometimes ten reals (four dollars). There are lots of other kids doing the same kind of work so it is very competitive.

Before selling jewelry, I worked in a fruit market. I didn't earn very much at all doing that, though.

I hadn't committed any serious crimes before [working in the fruit market]. I have robbed people and broken into a drug-store. But I only did it because I was skint [broke]. I think crime is just a way of surviving. But it's also about people who've got a nerve. I do feel really sorry for the victims of crime, though.

I know some people who earn a living as prostitutes. It's not cool for them. It hurts deeply, feeling that that is your life. They have to become hardened, to learn how not to feel too much.

My mother used to earn money at night, chatting up customers, as a woman of the night, a prostitute. Now she has registered for elderly assistance and receives a basic food basket each month. I love my mother more than anyone in the world. She hasn't got a mark on her, despite all her time in bars and brothels. She has had no formal education at all. She is just pure, from the heart.

When Mum got paid some compensation money from the government, she bought a little house in the favela at Engomadeira, and I went to live with her. While I was living there, I worked in a fruit market, for about two years. Working, no school. There was this Dona Vilma; she was like an auntie. She liked us. We would say we had walked all the way to school, and she would believe us. We were fond of her, too. She sometimes gave us one real. One day she asked me where I lived. I said Engomadeira. She said that her husband was opening a fruit shop there, if I wanted to work there. It was some time after, but it ended up working out."

Hamilton is not proud of some of the things he has done to get by on the streets, but he believes it was a necessary part of trying to stay alive.

CHILD LABOR

Street children are often forced to work to earn money either for themselves or for their families. Jobs include washing car windshields, shining shoes, selling souvenirs to tourists, and selling food. Because most of these jobs entail working long hours through the day, these children are unable to go to school, reducing their chances of getting a better job when they are older.

Wealthier Brazilians often employ street children to do odd jobs around their homes, such as gardening, exercising pet dogs, or cleaning swimming pools. Some older children move into the houses of the people they are working for and becoming servants. Girls are sometimes hired to become full-time maids or babysitters.

Children on the streets struggle to make a living, like this young boy who is selling ice cream.

Children as young as this group playing in a Rocinha favela can be vulnerable to the many threats on the streets of Brazil.

VULNERABLE TO VIOLENCE

Children are most vulnerable to danger when they first begin to live on the streets because they have not yet learned the ways of the streets. Perhaps surprisingly, one of these dangers is violence and abuse from gangs of other street children.

A child who is new to the streets might accidentally wander into an area of a city that is "owned" by a drug gang that uses street children to do their dirty work. Children on their own might also have something valuable that others want. Some older street children some-times inflict violence on younger children to enforce their authority over them.

Living on the Street

"We had a friend who was a bus driver—Viola. Because we used to beg on the buses, we got to know him. He'd let us on. He would pay us to clean the bus out—sweep it out and then rub this oil on the seats and stuff.

He would take us for lunch. I still see him around sometimes. He would do the Barra, Praça da Sé run. When we all got on that bus at Ibveji, it was right chaos; when we all got on together, we caused absolute mayhem! We'd get bus passes from Ibveji and then get away without using them. We'd save them up all week, so that we could get a hot dog and some pop with them or even to club together to smoke some cannabis. Anything for a bit of a party!

On the streets, it often got very cold at night. When the buses stopped, we'd stand behind them, next to the motor, where it was really hot, to get warmed up. We would sleep huddled up together for warmth, too. When I lived on the streets, there were lots of times without help, but never without hope.

I have always tried to make the best of things, to do the best I can under the circumstances. I'd go off to be alone, maybe down to the beach to have a bit of a think, forget, smoke, look at the sea.

When I was on the street, the police would wake us up. People usually gave us some breakfast (bread and milky coffee). Sometimes we woke up, and it was already sitting there beside us. Then we'd go off begging on the buses. We'd ask for

Hamilton has been fortunate to meet people who have wanted to help him, such as Nivaldo Ferreira da Silva (left). Hamilton will always be grateful to these people for their kindnesses.

leftovers in restaurants. In the afternoon, we might go and hang out at the beach. In Vitoria, there was this really nice lady; she used to give us fruit, juice, beans, and rice and chicken. Then we'd go off after money for our supper and breakfast and then look for somewhere to sleep."

SAFETY IN NUMBERS

Living on the streets can be lonely, and it is good to have friends around. Children on the streets often band together for protection. They can also work together during the day and then share whatever they have earned.

Finding the right place to sleep at night is critical for street children. The best places are open and public spaces. These are much easier places for one child to guard and watch while the others sleep. Street children also must make sure that they are not in an area controlled by another gang and to protect themselves from security guards and the police.

Safety in numbers is one of the fundamental laws of the street. Children usually take turns at watching out for danger.

MURDERED IN THEIR SLEEP

On July 23, 1993, eight street children, ages ten to seventeen, were killed when three masked gunmen opened fire on a group of fifty children who were sleeping beside the Candelaria Church in the center of Rio de Janeiro. The gunmen turned out to be policemen. One of the survivors of that attack was shot several times before the trial. Only one of the police officers was found guilty of killing the children. There was an international outcry, but the murders have not stopped.

In 2000, one of the witnesses to the Candelaria massacre was killed outside her house. Many believe that her murder was meant to warn others against testifying against police officers in similar cases.

A group or mourners carry the casket of one of the victims of the Candelaria massacre in 1993.

Living on the Street

"I used to knock about with Jau, Ricardo and Itamar; we went everywhere together. We'd go off and beg together in the streets. We'd get on the bus together; one would do one side of passengers, one the other side, asking for money. But if we saw someone getting some money out for us, first there got it! We'd swap sides if we saw an opportunity – whoever got there first got the money! It would end up in chaos!

Moabe—he's addicted to drugs now. If I had the money, I'd adopt him, take him in, and bring him up. He's a great kid. He's suffered a lot and [is] even worse now. What I want for myself, I want for the others, too, even more for those that were part of my childhood.

I was a little kid when I started living on the streets. I'd go out all over the place. I went all over Salvador; I really had a good time doing that when I was small. The kick of getting on buses and going to various places. Sometimes I'd fall asleep on the bus, and I'd end up at the final stop. I'd just jump from bus to bus begging for money, and then, when I got to the end stop, I'd spend it on a snack and some juice. It was all a big adventure.

I imagine how my life will be in the future a lot. One day I would like to live in the country, surrounded by green and nature. I want to meet someone special and have children one day. If I could go anywhere in the world, I think I would go to Disneyland."

Hamilton dreams of turning over a new leaf and going back to continue his education.

Children from poverty-stricken families can be found wandering hungry around the slums of Brazil's cities almost as soon as they can walk.

FACTS: WORK FOR STREET CHILDREN

In Brazil, it is illegal for children under the age of fourteen to work except as an apprentice. Many street children younger than fourteen must work to survive, however.

• The UN's International Labour Office has estimated that about 16 percent of all ten- to fourteen-year olds are working in Brazil.

• About 17 percent of all workers in Brazil are children or teenagers; in northeastern Brazil, that figure is nearer to 30 percent.

• About 80 percent of child workers earn less than minimum wage, which equals one dollar per day.

• Only 25 percent of child workers get help with education and social security.

• It is also estimated that nearly eight thousand Brazilian children are working in unhealthy or painful conditions at any time.

"He sleeps in the corner of the square,
Covered in cardboard,
Each day that passes,
He goes out in the street to earn his bread.
He doesn't know anything about
The crisis of this country.
Each day that passes,
Children, oh unhappy children.
Extermination No No No."

from a song called "Extermínio Não" ("Extermination No") written in response to the many death-squad murders of street children.

Many children on the streets of Brazil work up to fourteen hours a day just to earn enough for the day's food.

CHAPTER FIVE: A Better Life?

Despite all he has endured in his life so far, Hamilton has remained upbeat and enthusiastic about his future prospects. There is no doubt that he wants a better life than the one he is currently living. He is well aware that there is no future for young people on the streets—and that things such as drugs, prostitution, violence, and crime only succeed in damaging their lives and suppressing their true potential.

Hamilton now spends a lot of time in the Terreiro district where he can find work selling to tourists.

HAMILTON SAYS:

"I worry about the future. I don't want things to go wrong, I don't want to mess up my life. At the moment, I am looking forward to changing my lifestyle, to Carnival . . . and hopefully meeting a girl, the one for me. If I could have one wish, it would be that I could get out of this life that I'm in now and move on to better things."

JULIA SAYS:

"It is time for us all to question why the world is so unbalanced and what causes the extremes of poverty and wealth that we are becoming so accustomed to hearing about and seeing on TV. We can become informed about youth, about Brazil, about our world and become active in doing what we can, at home or elsewhere, to change attitudes for the better.

Like millions of other young Brazilians, Hamilton has had a difficult life so far. However, now living with his mother in the Rocinho district, he claims to be happier than he has ever been. Hamilton's goals include developing his jewelry business and going back to study as soon as he can."

YOUTH DETENTION CENTERS

Street children who have been arrested for petty crimes are not put into jail with adult criminals but are placed in Youth Detention Centers. Children who commit more serious crimes are placed in jails reserved specifically for young people.

In theory, youths will receive the appropriate care and be given the chance to get some education in these institutions. In fact, however, there have been accusations that guards who work in the centers have beaten children. Children can also be locked in their cells for several days without any exercise or the chance to meet others. The cells are often filthy, and sickness is common among inmates.

This inmate at Salvador's jail for minors was locked up for attempting to murder a boy for stealing his sneakers.

HELPING STREET CHILDREN LEARN

For many street children, education is the only way that they will escape from the streets and make new and better lives for themselves. They need schooling and job training to qualify for positions that make more money than the jobs they did on the streets. Many charities work to make sure that these young people have good educational opportunities. For example, ChildHope UK is working in the favelas of Rio de Janeiro to create opportunities for young people so that they can train for a job.

These children once lived on the streets. They are now enrolled in one of the many courses run by various charities. Their studies will help them find better-paying jobs.

PROTECTING THE STREET CHILDREN

Children on the streets of Brazil's cities are among the most vulnerable members of society. Not only do they have to look after themselves every day, but they also must face daily threats from death squads and corrupt police who are paid by businesses and local politicians to clear them off the streets. For many years, the Brazilian government did little to help street children. Many members of the Brazilian ruling class saw the children as little more than vermin or criminals.

It was not until the 1990s that the Brazilian government began to act to help protect street children. In 1990, congress passed the Statute of the Child and Adolescent. It was supposed to allow street children the "right to freedom, respect, dignity as a human being" and the "right to be in a public and community space." The statute also says that children can only be arrested if they are seen committing a crime, which was supposed to protect them from corrupt police. Drug gangs have exploited this change in the law by using children to smuggle drugs.

THE CHILD AND ADOLESCENT ACT

Until the Child and Adolescent Act went into effect, no child in Brazil, whether they were street children or not, had any rights that were written down in a law. The Statute of the Child and Adolescent made it clear for the first time not only that children needed special protection and consideration but also that they had the right to expect this special treatment. The act also compelled the Brazilian government to take particular care of children who are vulnerable— including street children.

The act called for the creation of two types of councils to ensure that the needs of young people are being met. The first type are Guardianship Councils, which were supposed to be set up all over Brazil to listen to the needs of individual children and make recommendations for how they could improve their lives. Local Children's Rights Councils were also supposed to be established. These councils were intended to decide on policies that affected children and distribute money to those who work with them.

These two councils have been set up in many parts of Brazil. In some parts of the country, however, they have not been established, or they do not have as much power as they are supposed to have. These areas are poorer than others in Brazil and cannot afford to run the councils. They also contain a larger number of children that need more help from the councils.

While there are some police who genuinely care about protecting the rights of street children, many more are employed by business owners to clear children off the streets by whatever means necessary.

Various government programs have tried to tackle the problem of substandard education in many parts of Brazil. The problem of poor education for many children still persists.

LEARNING OPPORTUNITIES

One of the main reasons why children do not go to school is simply because their families cannot afford to send them. Although education is free, the children can't earn money for their families while they are at school.

In 1991, the Brazilian government began to encourage street children to return to school. President Fernando Collor de Mello promised to open five thousand new schools for the children of poor families. By the time the president was removed after accusations of fraud in 1992, it was discovered that only twenty of these schools had been built and even fewer were open. In the end, only five thousand children benefited from this project.

In 1998, the new president, Fernando Henrique Cardosa, launched a program to get children living in poverty back to school. The program offered parents of poor children twenty-five reals (about ten dollars) per month for each child they sent back to school. This money was supposed to replace the money that the child would have earned on the streets. There have been reports that some parents are not getting the money that is owed to them or that they are keeping the money but still sending their children out to work in the evenings.

ERADICATING CHILD LABOR

Getting children back to school will help to make sure that they do not have to work to survive. The Brazilian government has made getting rid of child labor completely a priority. In 1998, the Brazilian government created the Program to Eradicate Child Labor (PETI). Its goal is to end child labor completely. By the end of 2000, PETI had helped hundreds of thousands of children escape work obligations or enforced work.

Shockingly, children on Brazil's streets can end up working as young as three or four years old. This girl makes her living by washing car windshields.

CHAPTER SIX: Those Who Help

Many aid organizations and charities that deal with children have been working with the Brazilian government trying to help street children. While some of these organizations originate in Brazil, others are international and work with street children all over the world. Some of these bodies are known as nonprofit social service agencies and include the Red Cross and Save the Children. These organizations rely on donations from individuals and funding from developed nations to do their work.

Poverty can drive hungry children to forage for food at the local dump. In hot climates such as Brazil's, rotten and decomposing food can be a breeding ground for bacteria and disease.

STREET CHILDREN AROUND THE WORLD

Countries that have been at war with neighboring nations or are fighting a civil war see an increase in the number of children who have become separated from their families while escaping from war. Some children find that their parents have died. In both cases, children often head toward the nearest town to find work and food and often end up on the streets. Countries such as Nepal and Ethiopia have street children as a direct result of civil conflicts.

Poverty and inequality also forces children onto the streets. As the gap between rich and poor continues to increase, the number of poor children on the streets has grown, particularly in developing nations but also in richer, usually more stable nations such as Russia and Romania.

CHILDHOPE AND ESTRELA

ChildHope UK was established in 1990 to defend the rights of street children around the world and provide opportunities for them to create a better future for themselves. It works with children in Africa, Latin America, and Eastern Europe. In Brazil, ChildHope works most closely with those children who are victims of violence or are involved in prostitution. Their work includes a young people's theater project in Brazil's favelas.

Founded in 1997, Estrela is based in Britain and works in the city of Salvador in

Brazil. The group works with youths and communities in Brazil and Britain to promote community, individual development, and intercultural understanding. One of Estrela's main projects is to support small-scale activities in Salvador that involve theater, art, or dance.

CULTURA EM MOVIMENTO

Cultura em Movimento (Culture in Movement) is a prominent cultural and arts organization based in Salvador, Brazil. The organization grew out of an activist organization called SOS Children of the Historical Center. SOS fought against the government program of the late 1980s that evicted people from their homes with the promise that houses would be returned to their residents once they were restored. This promise was only fulfilled for a small percentage of those affected. SOS rallied the people to rise up and fight against the restoration project, to say no to what was being offered. In time, the organization relocated to the Rocinha favela and evolved into a cultural movement, celebrating the rich cultural legacy of the region. Nivaldo Ferreira da Silva, also known as "Aluminio," leads Cultura em Movimento, which holds regular reggae music events. These occasions have become internationally renowned and include all people of the region, whether they live in houses or on the streets. An atmosphere of peace pervades these events, providing a haven from the aggressive elements of life on the streets.

THE NATIONAL MOVEMENT OF STREET CHILDREN

In 1985, political activists and people who worked with street children founded the National Movement of Street Boys and Girls (MNMMR). The goal of the movement is to encourage children to organize and look after themselves better while living on the streets. The movement includes about three thousand "street educators," who have reached tens of thousands of children. The street children are encouraged to form groups called a *núcleos*. The movement also makes sure that the 1990 Statute of the Child and Adolescent is never forgotten.

Living on the streets can be a lonely and desperate experience for children.

CASE STUDY: MOTHER CITY

Many of these organizations work in conjunction with the Brazilian government and also with local governments to provide support for street children. One project that has been funded by the government is Cidade Mãe (Mother City). This project is based in the city of Salvador in northeastern Brazil. The project tries to train young poor people so that they can find better-paid jobs and escape poverty. As well as providing training for young people who are not in school, Mother City also runs after-school clubs for those who are lucky enough to attend school.

Mother City is also concerned with reducing the number of fourteen- to eighteen-year olds who become addicted to drugs or become pregnant. The project provides health, sex-education, and counseling programs.

NUMBERS OF STREET CHILDREN

After events like the Candeleria massacre in 1993, Brazilians are slowly changing their minds about street children. More adults are realizing that these children need help rather than punishment for being poor. Hopefully, they will put more pressure on the government to do more for the children. Street children's lives will improve and their numbers on the streets will fall as long as the Brazilian government and aid organizations try to help them either directly or through their families.

Because the population of Brazil is continually growing, however, the number of street children might actually increase. The population is currently about 184 million. According to the United Nations, this figure is due to increase to nearly 250 million by 2050. This growth will be almost entirely due to more children being born rather than immigration. The growing population will put a strain on Brazil's schools, housing, jobs, and transportation. If the country cannot take this strain, then it is possible that

Most of the street children in Brazil are boys, but the number of girls seems to be constantly increasing.

the number of street children may actually go up rather than down.

MORE EDUCATION, LESS VIOLENCE

The Brazilian government wants the country to become a more economically powerful nation, with a stronger voice in the United Nations. This growth can only be accomplished through using the talents of all Brazilian people, young and old, rich and poor. Members of the Brazilian government know this cannot be achieved while there are huge numbers of poor and unskilled people in both the cities and rural areas. Providing educational opportunities is the most important way to help the poor.

Street gangs use guns and other forms of violence to settle arguments between different groups. The drug trade also makes it almost impossible to help young people out of poverty. The police forces often do nothing to tackle these two major problems. Guns, drugs, and police corruption must be eliminated before other government programs will really start to work.

MAKING LIFE IN BRAZIL FAIRER

In 2002, the Workers' Pary candidate for president and its founder Luiz Inácio Lula da Silva promised that he would give land to the landless poor. When he won, he began a series of reforms that included giving land to many thousands of people who did not own any land.

Reducing the increasing gap between rich and poor in Brazil will only happen if all future governments make sure that the benefits of economic growth are spread more evenly across all parts of Brazilian society. In the past, as the economy grew, the poorest members of Brazil did not gain as much as the wealthier ones. If poorer families become a little richer, then there is less need for their children to go out to work or for young people to be forced out onto the streets.

After the scandalous Candelaria massacre, the people of Brazil finally started to recognize that their country, and in particular their young people, were in the middle of a crisis.

Street children trying to earn a living selling souvenirs to tourists must compete against adults trying to sell the same goods.

HOW YOU CAN HELP

1. BUY FAIR-TRADE GOODS
Buying fair-trade goods helps ensure that farmers in poor countries are paid a good price for the crops they grow. Crops grown in Brazil include coffee and cocoa.

2. PARTNER WITH A SCHOOL IN BRAZIL
When your school is partnered with a school from another country, pupils from each school exchange letters and photos. If your school does not already have a sister school, ask your teacher to find out if there is a way to partner with a Brazilian school.

3. MAKE A DONATION
Many charities are working to make the lives of Brazilian street children better. You can make a donation to help them with their work. Always make sure you choose a registered charity so your money goes where you intend it to go.

4. SPREAD THE WORD
Many of the charities and organizations that work with street children can provide speakers to come to your school. Ask your teacher if he or she can help with organizing a talk.

5. TALK TO OTHER GROUPS
If you belong to a group like the Boy Scouts or Girl Scouts, then you can make links with similar groups in Brazil. Talk to your group leader about this. If you belong to a religious group, then you might be able to make contact with other religious organizations in Brazil. Discuss this with your religious leader.

Glossary

ABANDONED Deserted or left behind permanently.

APPRENTICE A person who is learning a trade or art from a skilled worker.

BROTHEL A building where prostitutes work.

CANNABIS Marijuana, an illegal drug that is usually smoked and produces an intoxicating effect.

CAPOEIRA A type of graceful and disciplined martial art that originated among Brazilian slaves and is still commonly practiced in Brazil and around the world.

CARNIVAL The most famous event of the Brazilian calendar, a party that takes place on the streets of Brazil's cities every February and lasts for five days. The end of Carnival was orginally associated with the beginning of Lent, a Christian observance.

CHOREOGRAPHED A composed sequence of dance steps and moves.

CIVIL LIBERTIES Rights of the individual that are part of living in a democracy; these rights include freedom of the press, speech, and assembly.

CONFLICT Serious disagreement, struggle, or fight.

CORRUPTION Acting dishonestly in return for money or personal gain.

DEATH SQUAD Name given to a group of police officers acting outside the law by killing street children. Death squads also kill people suspected of being criminals or who are political adversaries.

ECONOMY The way a country or people produces, divides up, and uses its goods and money.

ECOTOURISTS People who tour natural habitats in a way that reduces their impact on the environment.

ENFORCE Effectively cause something to happen.

EVICTED Legally forced to move from one's home.

EXPLOITED Derived benefit from something unfairly and at someone's expense.

FAVELA Shantytown or slum with houses made of cheap materials. The houses are often supported by poles because they are usually built on unstable ground, such as hillsides.

FORAGE Search widely for food or supplies.

GHETTO A part of a city where minority groups are often forced to live.

IMMIGRANTS People who move permanently to a foreign country.

MALNUTRITION Inadequate nourishment that often causes weakness and disease.

MASSACRE Indiscriminate and brutal slaughter of people.

MILITARY POLICE Uniformed police officers that operate in large groups.

NONPROFIT SOCIAL SERVICE AGENCIES Organizations that work to help disadvantaged people in various ways.

PERIPHERY The edge of something.

POLICIES Courses of action proposed by an organization or individual.

POVERTY LINE A level of income below which a family or indiviudal is considered poor according to government standards.

PROSTITUTE A person who exchanges sex for money.

PROSTITUTION The practice of engaging in sexual relations for money.

REFORMS Changes something for the better.

RESTORATION The action of renovating or restoring something that is in need of repair.

SALVATION Deliverance from sin by belief in religion, typically Christianity.

SAMBA Brazilian dance of African origin.

SCANDALOUS Something that is morally wrong.

SMUGGLE To move goods illegally into or out of a country.

STRIKE A work stoppage to force an employer to meet employees' demands.

TRUANT To stay away from school without permission from a parent or guardian.

UNDERNOURISHED Not having enough food for good health.

VERMIN Small common animals that are harmful to crops or carry diseases and are hard to get rid of.

VULNERABLE Exposed to the possiblity of being harmed, either emotionally or physically.

Further Information

CANADIAN INTERNATIONAL DEVELOPMENT AGENCY

Click on "Youth Zone" to get information about how to get involved in issues concerning children living on the streets around the world. This site also lists numerous opportunities to work, live, and study in devleoping countries.

www.acdi-cida.gc.ca/index-e.htm

CHILDHOPE UK

An international social service based in Great Britain, ChildHope is committed to working with children who are neglected by their families, communities, and governments and are the most vulnerable to violence, exploitation, and disease. Their work focuses on reducing violence against children and the impact of HIV and AIDS on orphans and other vulnerable children.

www.childhopeuk.org

ESTRELA UK

An organization based in Great Britain that works with youths and communities in Brazil and Britain to promote development for the disadvantaged and intercultural understanding. Estrela is involved with many projects that assist street children and promote more widespread understanding of the issues facing Brazil, such as setting up links between schools in Brazil and Britain; organizing talks and workshops on Brazil and street children in Britain; and assisting art- and music-based projects to develop the talents of street children.

E-mail estrela@atarde.com.br for more information

HUMAN RIGHTS WATCH: CHILDREN'S RIGHTS

This organization monitors systematic abuses against children around the world and works to end them. These abuses include child labor and prostitution, police violence against street children, and discrimination in education. The group works with local governments to expose mistreatment of children and to end it.

hrw.org/children/about.htm

NATIONAL MOVEMENT OF STREET BOYS AND GIRLS

The National Movement of Street Boys and Girls (Movimento Nacional de Meninos e Meninas de Rua, or MNMMR) was founded in 1985 in Brazil by activists and street educators who sought to empower and organize street children in their own environment.

pangaea.org/street_children/latin/mnmmr.htm

Index